Léon Bakst

THE DECORATIVE ART OF
LÉON BAKST

APPRECIATION BY
ARSÉNE ALEXANDRE

NOTES ON THE BALLETS BY
JEAN COCTEAU

TRANSLATED FROM THE FRENCH BY
HARRY MELVILL

DOVER PUBLICATIONS, INC.
NEW YORK

Published in Canada by General Publishing Company, Ltd., 30 Lesmill Road, Don
Mills, Toronto, Ontario.
Published in the United Kingdom by Constable and Company, Ltd., 10 Orange Street,
London WC 2.

This Dover edition, first published in 1972, is a republication of the work originally
published by The Fine Art Society, London, in 1913. The present edition is unabridged
except that the statements of ownership of the drawings, now largely obsolete, have been
omitted. The order and numbering of the illustrations have been altered with the purpose
of keeping all the color plates together. Two of the plates here reproduced in black and
white (present numbers 55 and 56) were reproduced in color in the original edition.

International Standard Book Number: 0-486-22871-1
Library of Congress Catalog Card Number: 73-187844

Manufactured in the United States of America
Dover Publications, Inc.
180 Varick Street
New York, N.Y. 10014

CONTENTS

LIST OF ILLUSTRATIONS

COLOUR

APPRECIATION

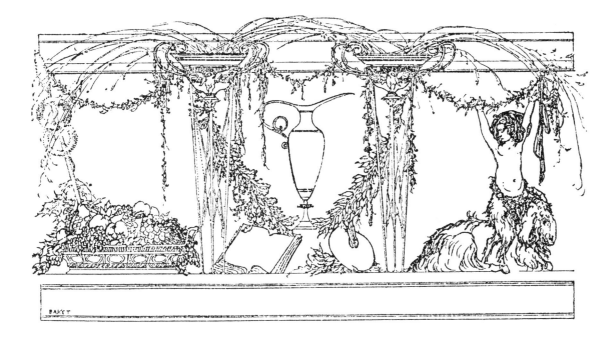

THE DECORATIVE ART OF
LÉON BAKST

The wonderful series of stage-settings that Léon Bakst has given to the world owe a great deal of their fascination to the strange blending of rich and sensuous beauty with a note of something sinister and almost menacing. From the first he was acclaimed a master of the harmony of line and colour *in movement;* that is one of his great secrets, and with each successive production his work has been more clearly recognised as an essential factor in, and an integral complement of, the enchanting inventions of the poets and musicians with whom he has worked.

This is the main reason of his success, and of the influence he has acquired, and this is why the present collection of his drawings has been made, to commemorate so remarkable a triumph of intelligence and fine taste.

It will be well to analyse this, even though the pleasure felt at the time may defy analysis. To reason about any delightful experience, far from diminishing one's recollection of it, actually makes it more vivid and permanent. Only during the performance must one give oneself up entirely to the joy of not attempting to understand it.

First let us consider the relation of this art of Léon Bakst's to the creations of the poets. We need make no excuse for discussing them first in an essay that is to treat mainly of music and dancing. " Honour to whom honour is due "; and besides it is the poor poet who is usually forgotten.

When the soul is flying through space on the wings of music, when the eye is ranging over incalculable distances to an ever-changing horizon, and all one's being is throbbing in sympathy with the hero in his loves and his sufferings, one is apt to forget that all is born of the fancy of an invisible and sometimes unknown person, who, though often very humble and very unhappy, in his moments of inspiration has seemed possessed of all human knowledge and all the secrets of Nature. Even these he has endowed with additional beauty. For one magic instant he can raise the dead and restore to the ancient gods their forgotten rites. He has even created new beings and new gods, such as mankind had never imagined. And, yet more wonderful, he has given us, in place of existent women, The Woman—that never yet has been. Now when a poet, by means of words, has in epic, idyll, or drama, brought his mind into contact with ours and fired our imagination, we begin to *see* before our eyes a whole world of colour and form. It is impossible when reading the history of Cleopatra, or of St. Sebastian, of Daphnis and Chloe, or a little poem of Theocritus, not to *see* the changing lights and shadows of the scenes and the movements and the gestures of the actors. There are no eyelids heavy enough to shut out this association of ideas, no nerves so insensitive as not to vibrate involuntarily. This is a fact, a physical phenomenon before which we are helpless—happily! But, in their turn, these visions which we were powerless to dispel elude us if we try to define them further. Then we find that no eye is alert enough to retain a distinct image of any definite moment we want to recall accurately, no nerves sufficiently sensitive to be able to respond again at will to the old vibration. The colours pale and disappear, and what we took for solid shapes were only changeful shadows. All this would be disheartening were it not that certain privileged men are to be found who, armed with simple and rudi-mentary forms of matter, can stay the immaterial in its flight, and give us back a lasting presentment of the illusive.   These men are the painters.   With a few touches and a few colours, they can re-incarnate for us the personages and the scenes that the poet has created—that we believed had shown themselves to us and then vanished.   They are such magicians that they have the power of making us see again these figures and colours *exactly* as we had half-seen them before.   Better still, they show us new ones which we must admit are more beautiful than the old ones, while we know that there is no danger of our losing them.   This is in itself a splendid gift, but it is not because he possesses it, in common with many other capable painters, that we admire and regard him as a profoundly original genius.

*   *   *

There are regions where words seem never to have lived—regions, in truth, where they could not live.

These are the realms of sound, the kingdoms of Melody and Harmony.   Music can make itself heard, while words either die away or increase in volume, but lose their precision.   Strangely enough, music, like poetry, also calls up before our eyes, whether they be closed or vacantly gazing into the void, forms that move swiftly and colours that scintillate even more rapidly.

But if we try to retain them, to recall them, we fail hopelessly.   It were useless for anyone to show us the Chevreul colour-circle, with its endless gamut of tones, and ask us to point out the colour that we had caught a glimpse of; we should remain utterly unable to find anything analogous even to our most certain and vivid impressions. And yet here again there exist certain painters who will put their finger on the tones that are equivalent to the sounds that moved us. I say certain ones only, for all cannot do it. Many have a sufficiently perfect sense of expression and pose, detail and gesture, to enable one to conjure up the personages who move through a poet's dream, but it is rarely indeed that we meet those who can evoke the sensations and scenes suggested by the *colour of music,* whether it be associated with poetry or no.

Most are content with the *colour of painting,* which is comparatively monotonous and uninteresting. Look, indeed, how a Watteau, a Prud'hon, a Delacroix stand out among the painters of their day. And the more those men who are not endowed with this special sense strive to exhaust all the possible combinations of their palette, the further they get from the real harmony of tone, the symphony of colour, and all the music of painting.

Léon Bakst has this gift. With the greatest economy of means he obtains the greatest sum of effect, and thus he realises an " orchestration " of colour in unison with the true colour of music. Does he wish to show us the divine haze of Greece shimmering in the sun, or to call up the glowing, poisoned splendours of the East? Is it the palace of Cleopatra that must be filled for us with an atmosphere of love and of death? Bakst can find all the silvery greens, the burning purples, and the dusky golds that are the very essence of life as it passes there. In his landscapes —I am conscious of the inadequacy of the word—he always knows what will give the sense of animation and vitality that is so necessary. He delights in the spots and splashes of colour that sparkle in his fields, his woods, and his palaces, that with every movement lend themselves to combinations that will be always varied, always vivid, and always harmonious.

His general colouring, always broad and simple, as I cannot too often repeat, allows an infinite play of modulations, and seems itself to vary in tone, in sympathy with the poem and the music.

That is another gift, rarer and more personal than the first. But this does not mean that we have said all we have to say as to what constitutes the originality of our artist. There is something else, something even more special to himself.

Beings, human or divine, tragical or playful, are called into existence. One Muse is satisfied.

They are shown in the environment of line and colour in which alone they could exist. Another muse has nothing further to demand.

A third remains expectant, no less formidable than the others, the Great Terpischore, as rhythmically perfect in the immobility of her repose, as in the wildest frenzy of her dancing, and she it is whom it is especially difficult to propitiate.

Oh, yes; I am perfectly aware that many excellent people believe that dances and Dancing are synonymous. They do not shudder with indignation when they see a row of young ladies in petticoats like muslin lampshades "faire trois petits tours et s'en aller" to the accompaniment of brutal rhythms and vulgar tunes. They call the Polka a dance, and do not realize that the Waltz only begins to be a dance when it is " chaloupée." They do not understand that the only dancing that is a fine art is of antique tradition and of Oriental origin, and that it is an expression of art, in that it is an expression of life itself, made passionate and beautiful, infinitely complex and varied.

Nowadays any attempts at diversity of rhythm and complexity of expression are banned in the so-called dances of the public dancing-halls or the Opera ballet (one and the same thing); or at least they were for a long time, though thanks to the unceasing efforts of a few artists, they may be said to have reappeared on the scene. It must not be forgotten that to certain women of genius, like Loie Fuller and Isadora Duncan, is due the revival and the appreciation of the sequence of rhythm and the expressiveness of pose. They earned the right to be considered, by all who have a sense of the beautiful, as true "priestesses of Terpischore." This phrase may raise a smile, it is so redolent of the bad days when dancing was a lost art: but if we carry our thoughts back through the centuries to the time when Dancing was regarded as the equal of Poetry and Painting, we shall understand how the dazzling intuition of Léon Bakst has continued and completed for us the work of restoring the Great Muse to her ancient honours, a work which her two priestesses had begun; and this in face of the strenuous opposition of the Philistines of their profession.

The problem was how to clothe this ballet, created by the alliance of Poetry and Music, so as to give their interpreters their due importance and invest the whole with fitting glamour and appropriate splendour. But no! this is not a problem to be solved, but rather a miracle to be wrought. The word problem implies a system to be worked out by argument. But to one who, like Bakst, *knows* how to clothe his figures, Historical, Mythical, or Tragic, in "danceable" dresses, to him no reason is necessary—he sees, creates, and accomplishes.

This, then, is what we find so intensely individual and new in his work; he has seen his costumes in movement, in the actual movement of the poem. In looking through any old ballet records you will find but a series of meaningless fashion-plate figures, whether they be labelled sylphs or witches, pages or village maidens. Their garments, suggested in flat washes, seem rather to imprison them than to clothe them. The body beneath is obviously of cork or calico stuffed with sawdust.

But worse still! Every face is alike. The Queen and her attendant, the love-lorn maid and her rival will, one and all, be the same impossible creature, differing only in some detail of her trappings.

This is to condemn the Theatre to a life of artificiality; this is to overlook the fact that if one is a creator of stage characters, and has the privilege of dressing them on behalf of a great poet or musician, one must not look on them as insipid, monotonous puppets, but delight in their individuality and love them as human beings.

This is why your traditional costumier, not having bothered himself to understand, expresses nothing, and why, as a rule, stage dresses are so little suited to those who wear them, if they have a vestige of temperament of their own.

What has struck us from the first on looking at Bakst's drawings is that, unlike the dull productions of the professional designer, his costumes seem to be the natural garment—the logical envelope, so to speak—of the figures that the painter has been at pains to understand and to bring to life.

If it is a frenzied Bacchante, supple and strong-limbed, who comes leaping by, her leopard skin and the vine tendrils in her hair are all a-quiver in unison with her dancing form; or a young Faun, furtively watching the nymphs he longs to pursue, he will be Faun from horn to hoof, from the nape of his neck to the tip of his tail. Now it is a Queen who advances, mysterious, weary, cruel; no borrowed splendour hers; her crown, her armlets, her necklace, even that awful veil that we would fain raise even at the peril of our life—never has she worn aught else. How often, on the stage, beneath the coronation mantle and diadem, have we recognised the landlady's daughter, to the infinite delight of the caricaturist in search of material. But with Léon Bakst, or artists like him, such a thing could never happen, because even a daughter of the people costumed by him becomes indeed a Queen; and if she is to appear as a daughter of the people, she is made to look like one—a more difficult achievement still.

The monstrous creatures that swarm in the marshes or roam the fearful forests are gnarled and moss-grown, and make our flesh creep, as they should do. The gods and goddesses tear themselves from their shrines, and descend from the Empyrean, whether they belong to the Greek Olympus or to the grand epics of India. All these Bakst has understood, evoked, and characterised with their proper forms and appropriate accessories; and even the attitude and gesture which explain their rôle and their nature.

These suggested attitudes and features, far from paralysing the actor or dancer by confining him to one single mood, on the contrary help all his logical impulses and efforts because they sum up his whole nature.

On a stage thus equipped there are no " super-numeraries," and this it is, perhaps, which at first alarmed more than one manager.

*   *   *

We have now, I think, analysed and rather closely defined the originality of Léon Bakst. Let us now consider more in detail the sequence of his achievements. We shall thus have said all that is necessary, and be free to study the wonderful reproductions of his drawings and water-colours which, while they revive our memories of the theatre, are in themselves finished works of art, precious and complete.

Léon Bakst was born in St. Petersburg in 1868; he studied at the School of Fine Art there, but his independent and exuberant nature soon tired of the routine prevailing in official studios. Is there, by the way, but one type of official studio in all Europe? He went to Paris in 1895 where, for three years, he was the pupil of Edelfelt, who was a native of Finland. He was then commissioned by the Russian Government to paint " The Arrival in Paris of Admiral Avellan," a work by which he is represented in the Museum at St. Petersburg; and several portraits by him were noticeable in the Exhibitions of the Société Nationale from 1902 to 1905.

It was only in 1906, however, that Bakst became known as a remarkable artist. Serge de Diaghilew had commissioned him to decorate the galleries and to arrange a " bosquet " (intended for the sculpture section) for the memorable Exhibition of Russian Art, which revealed to us the vigorous but unfamiliar and unsuspected talent of such men as Lewitzky and Somof, Borowikowski and Wroubel, Venetzianof and Alexandre Benois, Brullow and Léon Bakst.

From that time Bakst was recognised as a born decorator, a man who had a vocation for the stage. Though he had failed, at an earlier period, to find at St. Petersburg the teachers his genius required, he was to find in that city a field favourable for his first experiments and the opening of a career worthy of his energies. For his first efforts were the mounting and the painting of the scenery of " Œdipus at Colonus" and "Hippolytus" for the Imperial theatres at St. Petersburg.

It would be absurd to say that this was done without protest and strong condemnation on the part of connoisseurs, whose notions were upset by this new art and who tried to enlist public sympathy for their shocked and scared senses. There were alarms and excursions, and hard words were uttered. A nick-name was found for Bakst, who was called by a

Russian word which I don't know, but the meaning of which is *décadent*, whereas he was in fact drawing his inspiration from elemental sources. Finally the storm subsided; a few fervent admirers were found whose influence permeated and converted the crowd, and Paris did the rest.

The ballet "Cléopâtre" in 1909, an exhibition of water-colour drawings in the Bernheim Gallery; the "Scheherazade," "Narcisse," "Le Spectre de la Rose," "Thamar," "Daphnis et Chloë," "Le Martyre de Saint Sébastien," "Le Dieu Bleu," "L'Après-midi d'un Faune," "Hélène de Sparte," Oscar Wilde's "Salome," these, together with an important exhibition at the Pavillon de Marsan, are the rapid, brilliant, and decisive victories won by Léon Bakst. In this manner Léon Bakst's genius has contributed to the splendour of the stage and to one of the periodical and necessary emancipations of the art of the theatre.

*   *   *

It may seem that we have said nearly all there is to say on the development and merits of this painter and realiser of dreams, and we might perhaps conclude here, were it not that there is, in our opinion, a deeper and more recondite reason for his success, a reason greater even than his talent as a draughtsman and a colourist, great as it is. This reason has hitherto been little understood; we will give it as it occurred to our mind with haunting persistency while studying his water-colours.

We had a vivid recollection of a very curious, very important, and rather unnoticed picture in the Salon of 1906 to which Bakst had given the title of "Terror Antiquus." It represented as a statue and, at the same time, as a phantom the awe-inspiring Cypris, such as the archaic hewers of marble used to figure her even before the predecessors of Phidias had portrayed her as more humane towards Humanity. Her lips half open, with that ironical and cruelly placid smile which we cannot regard without fear, she pressed to her bosom, against the narrow folds of her drapery, the symbolic dove. Below her, and beyond her, as though seen from an immense height, lay the gulfs and steep promontories of Hellas; and on the lands thus spread out were besieged cities, and warriors in splendid armour fighting and wielding spear and sword in furious onslaught.

This awful intoxication of battle seen beyond the gigantic image of Love was an admirable symbol of Pagan antiquity, and we felt that the man who understood so well the omnipotent goddess, and the formidable heroes who slew each other for her sake, had the deepest comprehension of the Olympian ages. No wonder he is so familiar with the most insignificant of fauns and the humblest of dryads. No wonder he has so aptly recorded the deeds of the heroes. In the South of Russia, his native land, he found himself between Greece and the East, whose mysteries he fathomed and interpreted as only a painter could who was fired by enthusiasm and *furor artisticus*.

We can understand how easy it has been for him to revive the fauns of Attica and the shepherds who were the companions of Daphnis, and at the same time to depict—it could almost be said, with another hand—the Queen of Queens, Cleopatra, and the supreme dancer Salome.

And it is because of all this that his daringly brilliant art is also so much alive, for it is drawn from the very springs of life in Asia and in Greece. It is because of all this that he so deeply moves and delights us, for he has stirred in each of us the slumbering Pagan and the unconscious worshipper of deities, hidden from us by the twilight, but destined by nature to return to life in the dawn of some distant to-morrow.

ARSÉNE ALEXANDRE.

NOTES ON THE
BALLETS

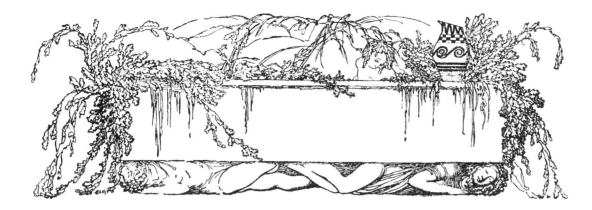

LE DIEU BLEU

J'imagine leurs yeux retroussés vers les tempes,
Lorsqu'au centre d'un chaud bassin,
Ils sortent du lotus qu'on voit sur les estampes
Arrondir son pâle coussin.

JEAN COCTEAU

What befell between the time night took the blue from the water and day put it back in heaven, is what the poet sets out to tell us.

Once upon a time, a young man wished to become a priest. After the prescribed seven days of prayer and solitude he was led into the temple, amid a great concourse of people and many ritual dances, to assume the saffron robe of the Servants of the Cult of the Lotus. But, just as he was divesting himself of his fine crimson tunic and tall white aigrette, the maiden he loved pushed her way through the guards and besought him to renew their lovers' commerce on the banks of the Ganges, where the Ibis drink.

21

If thou wilt free thyself from the fetters of mortality, fortify thy heart, think of Bouddha fighting against the seven arrows of desire, ponder on the jet of water which falleth back into the fountain after it hath tried in vain to mount to the pure air of paradise!

So it came about that the maiden tempted the young man, and the young man fell; but the priests would have none of it, and they seized the maiden, and left her alone with the giant tortoises, the sacred reptiles, and the monkeys.

She tried to escape, and, seeing light between the interstices of a golden trap-door, wished to find the way out. To her amazement, the trap-door yielded to her touch as if by magic.

It was but a cruel device of the sly old priests, for she found herself in a chamber teeming with the temple's monsters, swollen with honey, lambs, and nightingales, who slid out to meet her on their flabby bellies.

Knowest thou the weakness of the garden's stateliest rose, rooted to the earth by her stem, when assailed by an array of rampant slugs?

The maiden bethought her of the Goddess and implored the help of the Lotus. Then, of a sudden, there fell a great constraint upon all things, a brooding sense of mystery, which seemed to cow the monsters.

A phosphorescent light rose from the water. The Lotus opened, and from it came forth the Goddess seated beneath a dais of stamens.

The forefinger of her right hand was turned towards the surface of the basin, and, almost touching hers, another hand with forefinger uplifted, and then an arm appeared. This hand and arm were blue. And thus she brought the young God as her escort.

Thou canst not call in vain upon the Gods! The Goddess and the God were as translucent as the elements. She was like running water, and he like the blue of a blazing noonday.

At a signal from the Goddess, the blue God left the fountain and set about charming the monsters, a task he enjoyed like a schoolboy in a circus, and, when the last of the creatures had ceased to give the smallest trouble, he squatted in their midst with an air of childlike self-content.

Surely none could have felt terror at the engaging spectacle thus presented! And yet the priests were frightened out of their senses when they returned, armed with torches, for it is not always those who serve the Gods the most who are nearest to their mysteries.

After reuniting the lovers, the Goddess sank down once more into the pistil of the Lotus, and the blue God soared to the sky upon a magic golden staircase which unwound itself beneath his feet.

Verily, none can tell the true desires of the immortals!

L'APRÈS-MIDI D'UN FAUNE

Lys, et l'un de vous tous pour l'ingénuité.

S. MALLARMÉ

Here we must not look either for the deliberate audacity or classical correctness of treatment, which its detractors on the one hand, and its partisans on the other, claim to have detected in it. It is merely an incursion into the domain of plastic art on the part of a young barbarian, whose genius has been recently on a voyage of discovery in the museums, and found there fresh inspiration to gratify his modern yearning to make dancing reflect every phase of thought.

A faun plays the flute, drinks milk, looks at the sun through the leaves, and, sniffing the air, scents there an unknown presence, which, stooping from his rocky vantage-ground, he sees to be that of a group of nymphs. At sight of him all take to flight but one. He knows not why, and, in his awkward fashion, tries to woo the nymph, who, evading him, leaves in his grasp a scarf, which he carries to his retreat and winds ardently round himself.

Such is the story, which seems almost childish in its simplicity. The faun, elusive being midway between the human and the animal, has consciousness of nothing beyond his figs, his honey, his grapes and his flute. As he smoothes with his tongue his jaw —piebald like a horse-chestnut—his quaintly fascinating face seems to resent the weight of the horns upon his head. Could we hear him, one imagines he would laugh and bleat almost in the same breath, and all the while his wrinkled brow attests his yearning to cross the border that separates instinct from intelligence. He shows us more than "the nebulous" and less than "the luminous nucleus" of which Monsieur Bergson tells us.

I must be forgiven if I overstep a poet's licence in speaking of Monsieur Nijinsky's creation. This space would not suffice to do more than touch upon the salient features of any of them, much less of this one, which is more entirely his own than any other. To watch closely his portrayal of the faun is a revelation. Listening, or looking, amused, perplexed, or passionate, he remains perfectly poised on the line that divides the boy from the beast, and every movement of the ears, the eyebrows, the chin, the lips, the knees plays its part in the absolute illusion of the whole.

The scenery, or rather Monsieur Bakst's decorative back-cloth, I do not consider one of the artist's happiest efforts.   It can best be described as a piece of studied " stylisation," to use a hateful word.

As respects the dresses, on the other hand, the fluid draperies and plaited golden tresses of the nymphs, and the sandals of the faun make their appeal by the life which informs their archaic conventionality.

CLÉOPÂTRE

Bel Ermite! Bel ermite!

G. FLAUBERT

Cléopâtre remains to my mind one of the most satisfying productions of the Russian ballet. In it no one particular star outshines the constellation. Scenery, action, dancing seem to vie with each other in self-effacement, and the wonder of each unit to spring from the whole with which it blends to such perfection. From the appearance of the little Pyrrhic archer to the silent passing of the great galley, the story unfolds itself with such relentless clearness that one asks oneself if the silence of the action does not result from the ears' ignorance of the language of its characters. The music chosen to accompany it, hotly sensuous throughout, now floating like a cloud of grasshoppers, now grim as pythons interlaced, now oily as the course of old Nile itself, conduces to that special sensation of being adrift in time and space experienced by Wells's hero, whose delight at achieving his excursion into the past was counteracted by his anxiety as to the possibility of return. This ballet is too well known, and Monsieur Bakst's pictures are too suggestive, for me to add anything in the way of description, but I must try to give an impression of our first glimpse of Madame Ida Rubinstein who chose Cléopâtre for her first appearance. That impression is based upon some notes jotted down at the moment, and I can but trust that a vividness, of which memory is incapable, may atone for their incoherence.

. . . Then appeared a long ritual procession. First, musicians, who drew from their tall oval lutes full mellow chords, like the breathing of reptiles, and flute players with angular gestures, who blew from their flutes such a gamut of piercing notes, shooting up and down the scale so shrilly, that human nerves could scarcely bear the strain. Then followed, like figures in terra-cotta, fauns with long white manes, and slim maidens with sharp elbows and eyes without profiles, and all the equipage of a royal galley. Finally, balanced on the shoulders of six stalwarts, a kind of chest of gold and ebony was born aloft. A negro youth kept circling about it, touching it, making way for it, urging on the bearers in his zeal.

* * *

The chest was placed in the centre of the temple, its doors were opened, and from it was lifted a kind of glorified mummy, swathed in veils, which was placed upright on ivory pattens. Then four slaves subjected it to a marvellous manipulation. They unwound the first veil, which was red wrought with lotuses and silver crocodiles, the second, which was green with all the history of the dynasties in golden filagree upon it, the third, which was orange shot with a hundred prismatic hues, and so on until they reached the twelfth, which was of indigo, and under which the outline of a woman could be discerned. Each of the veils unwound itself in a fashion of its own : one demanded a host of subtle touches, another the deliberation required in peeling a walnut, a third the airy detachment of the petal from the rose, and the eleventh, most difficult of all, came away all in one piece like the bark of the eucalyptus tree.

The twelfth veil of deep blue released Madame Rubinstein, who let it fall herself with a sweeping circular gesture, and stood before us, perched unsteadily on her pattens, slightly bent forward with something of the movement of the Ibis' wings, and sick with waiting, for within her dark retreat she had felt, as we had, the effect of the sublimely enervating music of her retinue. On her head she wore a little blue wig with short golden braids on either side of her face, and so she stood, with vacant eyes, pallid cheeks, and open mouth, before the spell-bound audience, penetratingly beautiful, like the pungent perfume of some exotic essence.

*   *   *

It is a wonderful experience to assist at the draping of Madame Rubinstein before the curtain rises. Silent stage-hands and " supers " form a respectful circle round her, and melt gradually away as she disappears beneath the wealth of veils.

*   *   *

One night I had the honour to escort Madame Rubinstein for the process, for she cannot walk alone upon her pattens, and, as I felt the light weight of her trembling palm in mine, I thought of Flaubert's Cleopatra with her blue hair, her rapid breathing, her delicate discomfort.

*   *   *

Disposed as I already was to admire Rimsky-Korsakoff's music, Madame Rubinstein has fixed it in my heart, as a long blue-headed pin might impale a moth with feebly fluttering wings.

SCHÉHÉRAZADE

Tu ne me trompes jamais ô mon inquiétude.

HAFIZ

The heavy atmosphere of the harem is charged with impending tragedy, the swift retribution awaiting deception and desire. How should it be otherwise? Are not these fresh young flowers, born at dawn amid the silken cushions, predestined to die before nightfall? The sting of great secret storms is in the air, lashes the senses, fans the frenzy, precipitates the inevitable end. At the beginning, from out all the dull green depths of the opulent prison-house, is heralded the approach of the catastrophe. Nay, it is already there. It comes in the light of a deliverance, and, though there is nothing to reveal the exact manner of its coming, the tension is so great we know we have not long to wait for it.

The Sultan, caparisoned by his eunuchs, surrounded by his women, like some gorgeous pheasant with his mates fluttering about him, goes forth to war. The trumpets sound. Zobéide, his favourite, sick at the thought of the separation, sinks swooning to the ground.

The master has gone. Bereft of his presence, the women run about curiously examining every nook and cranny, adjust and readjust first their dainty shoes, and then their gauzy draperies, powder their faces and darken their eyelids, and then beg the chief of the eunuchs to open three blue doors whose giant golden key hangs from his girdle. He fears to consent, but bribes succeed, where entreaties fail, in breaking down his resistance, and he yields. From the first mysterious chamber, decked out in pearls and plumes, come forth negroes, arrayed in rose-colour, and from the second more negroes, arrayed in amber. On the threshold of the third, Zobéide crouches in expectant ecstasy as her comrades rejoin their lovers. Here the chief of the eunuchs pauses terror-stricken, but, under the gaze of his mistress's pleading eyes, he opens, and her lover springs out, in dress and demeanour first among his fellows, as she is queen among her women. His white teeth flash in his grey-black face, and he reels like some young animal blinded by the light after a long darkness. Naked to the waist, his garment of iridescent gauze glints like fish-scales in the sun. He bears off Zobéide in his arms.

* * *

Then begins an orgy of mad caresses, while, before the couples prone on the divans, a long procession passes. First, men in red and orange, with blue sugarloaf caps, balancing pyramids of fruit like conjurors, then cupbearers in pink and prune, and last, a string of girls playing on tambourines, intertwining its way through the harem. Meantime, the negro boy and Zobéide go through the whole gamut of fond and foolish looks and ardent gestures known to lovers, and more beside, till, at a signal from Zobéide, begins a wild, whirling, shattering dance, in which all join and which her lover dominates in a series of exultant bounds.

Then the Sultan returns. His brother, who has been with him and suspected mischief was afoot, has persuaded him to see for himself. At first the dancers do not realize the dread presence, turned to stone, in their midst, but when they do, panic runs through them like fire through chaff, and terror reigns in the harem, where negroes, women, and eunuchs are done to death. Heads overhang the marble steps they crimson, four soldiers slaughter the chief of the eunuchs, and the negro boy, dragged it may well be from the shelter of a great incense-burner, gets a sword-thrust in the face, and dies in long spasms like a bow first slowly strung and then as slowly relaxed.

Then ensues a great silence in the harem. Chastisement has been meted out to all but one—Zobéide, and her lord, moved by her tears, is of a mind to pardon her when his brother stumbles on the body of the negro boy. The Sultan's rage rekindles. He orders his guards to kill her, but she slips from their grasp, and, piercing her heart with her own dagger, drags herself to die at the feet, not of her lover, but of her lord, whereat the Sultan feels a great loneliness, and buries his face in his hands.

*　　*　　*

" Schéhérazade " is brought to a close on a poignant note from the violins, which seems, appropriately enough, to try to soar above the limits of the register.

Monsieur Bakst's water-colours, which alternate with these pale pages as brilliantly as do the vivid eyes with the grey feathers of the peacock's tail, render far more expressively than they can the glaring passion revealed in this exotic fairy-story of the irresponsible and the irreparable.

NARCISSE

*Son étrange folie continua jusq'aux
enfers, où il essayait encore de se
regarder dans le Styx.*

OVID

In a drama to be enacted in a setting such as this, water could not but play a dominant part. All around a spring keeps the earth perennially moist and nourishes a wealth of fungous vegetation. The shining green branches hang heavy from the trees like stalactites from the roof of a grotto and the sun scarce penetrates their dank luxuriance. Here, where the water laps beneath the image of the gods, is surely a sweet retreat for shepherds from the dog-days in the torrid country one divines beyond, sweet and yet dangerous in its sweetness, like a cup of cold water quaffed too fast.

And hither hie them shepherds with their hats thrown back from their brows and all the maidens from the eclogues, and with them, but a thought aloof, Narcissus, his narrow face held forward like the heart of the narcissus flower, his hair its pollen, his tunic its short white petals, the green thong round his leg its stalk. He sports and dances with one and all but looks at none.

" Claudite jam rivos pueri." "Déjà Vesper s'allume." The dusk is at hand. The shepherds drive home their flocks from the pastures. Silence has fallen on the velvet earth when Narcissus, after a surfeit of song and dance and laughter, returns alone to slake his thirst, and, kneeling on the damp moss, bends forward to drink.

There are evenings succeeding days of perfect calm when, after the light has ceased to outline every plant and pebble in a pool and before the coming of the darkness, the surface of the water is so smooth and glassy that no mirror can reflect with like precision.

And so Narcissus sees Narcissus. A cry escapes him and, as it strikes the rampart of the rock beyond, Narcissus hears Narcissus call.

Echo appears, fleeting and fragile as a wave of sound, to repeat to the youth the call addressed to her, and has but to catch sight of him at the water's edge to fall in love with him.

Narcissus tries to reach his brother by thrusting his arm into the pool, ruffles the surface and shatters the reflection. Fearing he has frightened him away, he calls him back tenderly by his own name. "Narcissus!" Echo imploringly calls back.

Surely there could not be a sorrier game of cross-purposes than that, in which Echo, the Spring and Narcissus thus find themselves engaged!

First, Narcissus gives the water little timid pats like a cat after an ever-wary fish, then lays his face so close he wets his cheek, then, after plunging in to the waist to find his double, only stirs the mud and can see nothing. The phantom thus seems lost to him for ever and he runs from side to side uttering childish plaints, which Echo just as plaintively repeats, till, at length returning to the pool, he finds the youth once more and looks upon his face in silent ecstasy.

Troubled by the eeriness of the dusk, the heavy breathing of the carnivorous plants, the croaking of the frogs and the toads' little hydraulic flute, poor abandoned Echo, her face bathed in tears, retreats backwards from her unhappy love, and Narcissus is alone once more.

The figure in the water becomes less and less distinct and Narcissus, to approach it, stretches himself out on the very edge of the grassy bank, heedless of the stains on his fair white garment or the muddy moisture on his naked limbs.

Thence he imperceptibly melts into the water, slanting downwards with the voluptuous easy grace of some young seal, and then, before the eyes of those mysterious denizens of the marshes, who grow cryptogamous in the slime, there rises from the midst of the pool a tall flower fashioned of the gold of his hair, the green about his leg and the white of his tunic and the flower has for its heart the mad gentle face of the shepherd-boy.

LE
MARTYRE DE S. SÉBASTIEN

Un nouveau signe est dans l'espace.

G. D'ANNUNZIO

What a delightful disproportion there is between the youth from the Florentine frescoes and his house! Both seem so scrupulously exact, and yet it appears so impossible to imagine the one getting into the other. Madame Rubinstein strikes the ear as a primitive picture strikes the eye. There is the same noble awkwardness, the same precise breadth of treatment, the same shy charm, though I dislike comparisons of the sort, (for if Madame Rubinstein recalls early Italian paintings, it is because all impressive works of art are apt to have a family likeness). In any case, she suggests some saint from a stained-glass window who, suddenly called to life, and still trammelled by the thought of his translucent immobility, has not yet grown accustomed to the newly-bestowed gifts of speech and gesture. She gives that impression throughout—when she says with childlike gentleness to Diocletian that he has been a generous master; when she calls upon the cruel kindness of her comrades in arms; when, in her intoxication of faith, she counts the glowing keys of her deliverance, and when she hangs, pierced by the arrows, against the tree, like the wreck of some gallant ship entangled in its rigging.

In the second act, which is one sustained cry of passion, the very quality of her breaking voice subtly indicates the passage, under its stress, from boyhood to maturity.

Throughout the five long acts, how admirably she alternates the feverishness, the ecstasy, the struggle, and the triumph of " L'Athlète du Christ " ! From the beginning, where she suggests a tall stately torch, to the end, where she is but a great flame dying in a pool of wax, every attitude seems to stand out from the air around it in sharper relief than if it had been cast in bronze.

Madame Rubinstein can afford to disdain further incense : but one cannot but dwell on certain aspects of her presentment of Saint Sebastian—her rapt attention as, encircled by the blue cohort of Emesa, she gazes at the twin prisoners, resting her arms in their sleeves of green velvet on her bow, her fine head crowned by the small cornucopia of her helmet: her inspired aloofness from her surroundings: her mystic walk: the look of stern tenderness with which she draws the unhappy mother, all unwilling, to the feet of the melodious martyrs, and, more than all, her wonderful dance, where, her armour aglow, her legs scorched, her toes seared, she treads the red embers as lightly as though they were, in fact, a magic carpet fashioned of the miraculous lilies in the blue arcades beyond. There are intonations, too, one must recall—her boyish cries to her companions to follow her when she discovers the magic chamber after the carnage of the idols, and her recital of the slave's beatitude, when her voice seems to come from out those starry depths which Monsieur Bakst has realized for us, behind the great doors against which she leans in radiant fragility.

HÉLÈNE DE SPARTE

Elle brodait sur une toile lisse et blanche comme l'albâtre les combats que les Troyens avaient subis pour elle.

HOMER

One of Monsieur Bakst's special gifts is his power to create at the beginning a tense and anxious expectancy by which the eventual enthusiasm is immeasurably enhanced. His effects are never produced in the way we anticipate, and the wonder, born of our surprise, gives us the nervous shock necessary to stir our emotions, the humble satisfaction of acknowledging a defeat which brings us the sweets of victory, the realization of a dream become reality. Monsieur Bakst told me once that he forces himself to live entirely with the characters whose atmosphere he has to create, until they themselves project that atmosphere upon him and dominate him by it, as Catherine Emmerich was dominated by the byways of Jerusalem and the briars of Golgotha. Therefore, as the passive " subject " of a trance his sincerity should not be called in question, and I will look no further than his obedience to a controlling influence for a reply to the critics of his " Helen of Sparta." He saw Pollux owner of a few flocks, king of a rugged, straggling township, dry with drought in the dog-days, and knee-deep in mud after rain. He saw his soldiers, like scorpions in their black harness, grouped one above the other on the rocky path leading up to his compact little palace, and his subjects like a swarm of multi-coloured ants in the open space below; he saw the low gate which leads to the plain beyond, and through which, on foot, to the strains of snuffling shawms and braying bag-pipes, and with some simple semblance of state, there enters a Helen, herself so simple that the heart swells with respectful tenderness at her approach. I shall never forget it. She seemed the embodiment of love and death. As each of her women had made their entry, one asked oneself, " Can this be she? " and then at last she came, not so very different from the others, and defying legend with her dark tresses, but announced by the sublime illusion of the truth, less stately, indeed, but far sweeter than one had looked for, and recalling her of whom Athenæus tells us:

"Chez Ménélas le jeune Télémaque et le jeune Pisistrate furent tellement intimidés d'être à la droite et à la gauche d'une personne aussi célèbre qu'ils ne parlèrent ni ne mangèrent du repas."

Therefore, prompt as I should be to curse a clumsy illustrator who had upset my childish hero-idols by drawing them too definitely, and divesting them of their halo of divine uncertainty, I am doubly grateful to Monsieur Bakst for having ventured for me into the vague, and brought back from it three personalities so different from what I expected, and yet so perfectly in tune with the primitive poetry of Lacedæmon.

DAPHNIS ET CHLOÉ

Daphni, tuum Poenos etiam ingemuisse leones
Interitum montesque feri silvaeque loquuntur.

VIRGIL

Everyone is familiar with this romance of a rococo Arcadia, recalled to us, as it is, by innumerable pictures which reproduce its leading incidents from the elaborate modesty of Daphnis' bath, while Chloe slyly looks on, to the suggestive entanglement of the four feet overhanging the edge of the grotto—the typical gallantries, which were such a sheer delight to the artists of the eighteenth century.

The lovers' sighs among the sheep, the pirates' brutal irruption, the least terrifying of storms succeeded by the most perfectly curved of rainbows, form an ideal framework for scenery which is suave and grim by turns, for dainty dresses which might have been designed by Ovid, and rags corroded by sea-iodine.

46

Monsieur Bakst has shown us a fearsome glimpse (between two mossy glades straight out of the eclogues) of the rugged creek where the pirates chain up poor Chloe while they indulge in their rough horse-play, and nothing could provide a more delightful contrast to their gruesome gambols than Daphnis' dance, tinkling and twinkling dew, or the ever-breaking garland of the most Latin of farandoles.

Do the pirates really exist, or are they the creations of a nightmare?—and those metallic goddesses? and the great god Pan?   May not the whole thing more likely be a figment of Daphnis' dreaming fancy?

My first impression of the Russian Ballet was, if I remember right, " Le Pavillon d'Armide."   Their thrilling dances then gave me a sharp pang of yearning to get a closer view of things immeasurable and unattainable, such as no poem of Heine's, no prose of Poe's, no fever dream has ever given me, and, since, I have invariably had the same sensation, at once sub-conscious and acute, which I attribute to the silent and nebulous precision of all they do.

" Daphnis et Chloé " ends with an awakening which suggests exactly the requisite degree of dazzled disillusion.

LE CARNAVAL

On soupait chez ce vice-roi.

MEILHAC ET HALÉVY

Thanks to the glowing warmth of Monsieur Bakst's inspiration, a dip into the near past for the first time fails to chill. These masks wear so bright a smile, the glimpse we get of this carnival, as we look back at it over our shoulders, is so full of colour that these gentlemen in nankeen pantaloons and these ladies in spensers, have none of the depressing effect associated with the anæmic reconstitutions dear to the ultra-pure and refined. Here we are miles removed from the short-sighted individuals who, in their inability to descry either the noble ruins of remote antiquity, the definite present, or the nebulous future, ransack the cupboards of a dull, drab yesterday. We have instead, inset, as it were, between pictures of the Nile and of the Eurotas, a rapid daguerrotype of one of those old stereoscopes which presented to our gaze fops with fob-chains paying their addresses to fair creatures in crinolines seated on unseductive ottomans.

It would be useless to attempt to describe this mysterious medley of imitation and improvisation, this succession of dances and dancers, each deriving so impeccably from dusty, dissolute days that are gone; these ladies with their short gloves, and wrists beribboned like their ankles, their braids and ringlets peeping out from under coal-scuttles and camellias, and their escort in plush cutaways and Hessian boots, white stove-pipes, and fine frilled shirts. What it behoves us to do is to try to fix an impression of Monsieur Nijinsky's presentment of the ballet's central figure.

Half Hermes, half harlequin, cat and acrobat by turns, now frankly lascivious, now slyly indifferent, and all the time the schoolboy up to every trick the turned-down collar of his dress suggests, as emancipated from the control of the laws of gravity as he is mathematically exact in the elaboration of his antic graces. The embodiment of mischief and desire, arrogance and self-satisfaction and a hundred things beside, with the drollest little nods of his head and strange sidelong glances from the shelter of his lids, one shoulder held higher than the other and the cheek bent to meet it, his left hand on his hip, his right palm outstretched, Nijinsky danced his way through "The Carnival" to the din of uninterrupted applause.

SALOMÉ

Long ago, at a period when the glamour of the unusual still sways "unhardened youth," I read Oscar Wilde's play, and I confess I was prejudiced against it by the recollection of a farrago of symbolism and verbosity characteristic of the age of counterfeit in which Wilde in England and Huysmans in France shone so brilliantly. Painters and poets have combined to endow the dancing princess with a halo of hysteria, and the crown of chrysoprase thus bestowed looms pale indeed beside the prismatic depths of Mallarmé, the genuine if barbaric gold of Flaubert, or even the tinsel gauds of Jules Laforgue.

The celebrated Salome in Rouen Cathedral is full of thrilling possibilities for those who have eyes to see. The determined little lady who can walk on her hands like any ragamuffin must surely know how to distract kings distraught and saner men beside.

Realizing that to resort to "extremities" is the only way to ensure an immediate reward, she would naturally substitute for the problematical process of slow seduction a short, sharp somersault!

In this connection, there is a story that Oscar Wilde was so much impressed by an acrobat who danced on her hands at the "Folies-Bergère," that he said to Meredith, "I must engage her! My Salome must walk on her hands like Flaubert's!"—an acknowledgment of indebtedness to a most worthy inspiration!

On the other hand, Aubrey Beardsley's charmingly pretty sister told me that "Oscar" himself never intended his "Salome" to be taken too seriously, and certainly her brother's famous illustrations, depicting Verlaine winking and the author tucked away in the moon, go far to substantiate the theory.

In any case, I found the play theatrically very effective, (in spite of certain absurdities attributable both to the author and the epoch), and revealing throughout the humour of "Troilus and Cressida."

What struck me most was the vein of social satire underlying it all. One felt Wilde to be a man of the world, obsessed by the importance of its ways. Indeed, the play might have had for its motto his own phrase: "To be in Society is merely a bore; to be out of it simply a tragedy." The Tetrarch is delightfully snobbish in his allusions to Cæsar: the princess is as preoccupied as if she were preparing a " parlour-trick " : Herodias has the all-embracing eye of the really experienced hostess: and one can imagine exactly what the smart young ambassador will say on his return from Rome.

The scenery is, to my mind, among the most appropriate we owe to the genius of Monsieur Bakst. The courtyard is surrounded by tortuous paths, worn unevenly by unsteady feet; the excessive size of the moon explains the exaggerated importance attached to it by all these moon-struck people; the exceptionally deep-crimson ramblers cling helplessly to the walls, and the awning recalls a thundercloud streaked with lightning. From their sordid debauch the guests stagger on to a terrace which overlooks the gutter, redolent of rotting rose-leaves, and registering, presumably, a far higher temperature than the reeking scene of revel they have left. Can one wonder, then, at the peculiar character of the post-prandial entertainment provided?

I had hoped to have the gratification of seeing Madame Rubinstein dance on her hands. She suggested many wonderful things, from an arrow to an antelope, but she did not dance on her hands! I am bound to add that that fact did not prevent her duly receiving the promised reward.

ILLUSTRATIONS

PLATE 1   LE DIEU BLEU: A Young Rajah

3 BAÏADÈRES avec paun
DIEU BLEU

BAKST
1911

PLATE 2 LE DIEU BLEU: Bayadère with a Peacock

PLATE 3   LE DIEU BLEU: Nijinsky in the Title Rôle

PLATE 4   LE DIEU BLEU : A Negro

PLATE 5   Le Dieu Bleu : Bayadère

PLATE 6   Le Dieu Bleu: The High Priest

BAKST
1911

DIEU BLEU
Pateau d'un
pour Jacrifice

PLATE 7   LE DIEU BLEU : An Attendant at the Sacrifice

BAKST
1911.

PLATE 8   LE DIEU BLEU: La Fiancée (Mme. Karsavina)

PLATE 9   LE DIEU BLEU: A Pilgrim

PLATE 10   Le Dieu Bleu : A Young Prince

PLATE 11   Le Dieu Bleu : Bayadère

PLATE 12   Le Dieu Bleu : Scenery

BAKST

PLATE 13   L'Après-midi d'un faune: The Faun (M. Nijinsky)

PLATE 14   L'Après-midi d'un faune: A Nymph

PLATE 15   L'Après-midi d'un faune: A Nymph

PLATE 16   L'Après-Midi d'un Faune : Scenery

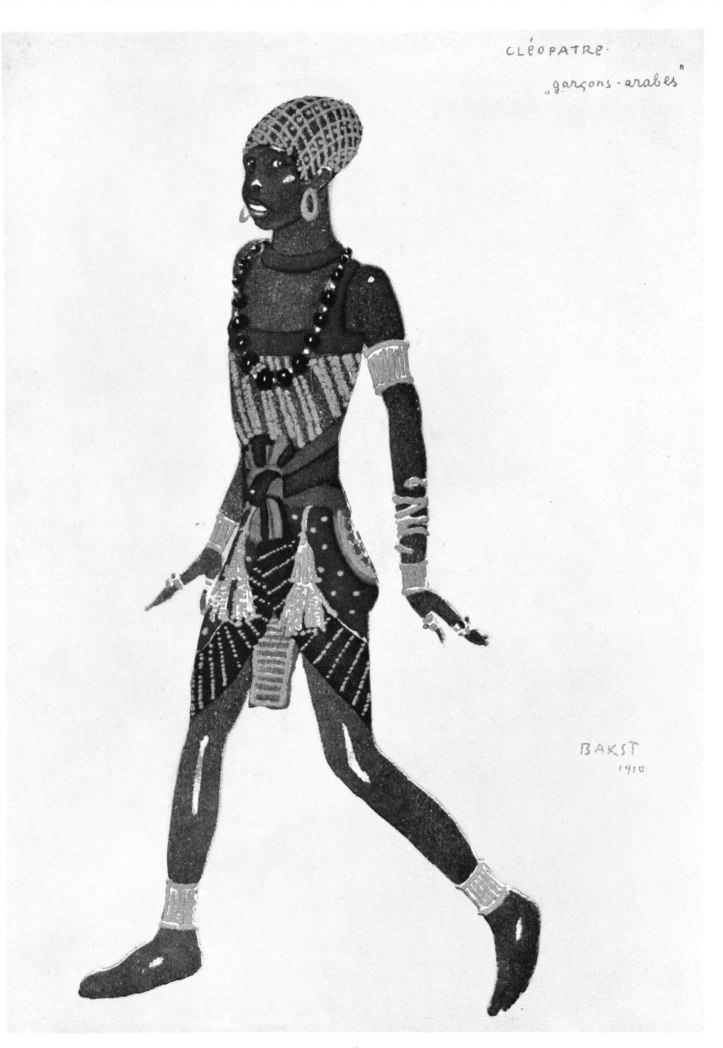

CLÉOPATRE.
„garçons-arabes"

BAKST
1910

PLATE 17   CLÉOPÂTRE: A Negro Boy

PLATE 18 CLÉOPÂTRE: A Jewish Dancer

à mon ami André Saglio
1909 Paris

BAKST

PLATE 19   CLÉOPÂTRE: A Syrian Dancer

PLATE 20   CLÉOPÂTRE : Sketch for Scenery

PLATE 21   Schéhérazade: An Odalisque

PLATE 22   Schéhérazade: A Young Man

PLATE 23   SCHÉHÉRAZADE: A Eunuch

PLATE 24   SCHÉHÉRAZADE : First Sketch for Scenery

PLATE 25   SCHÉHÉRAZADE: La Sultane Bleue

PLATE 26   SCHÉHÉRAZADE: An Odalisque

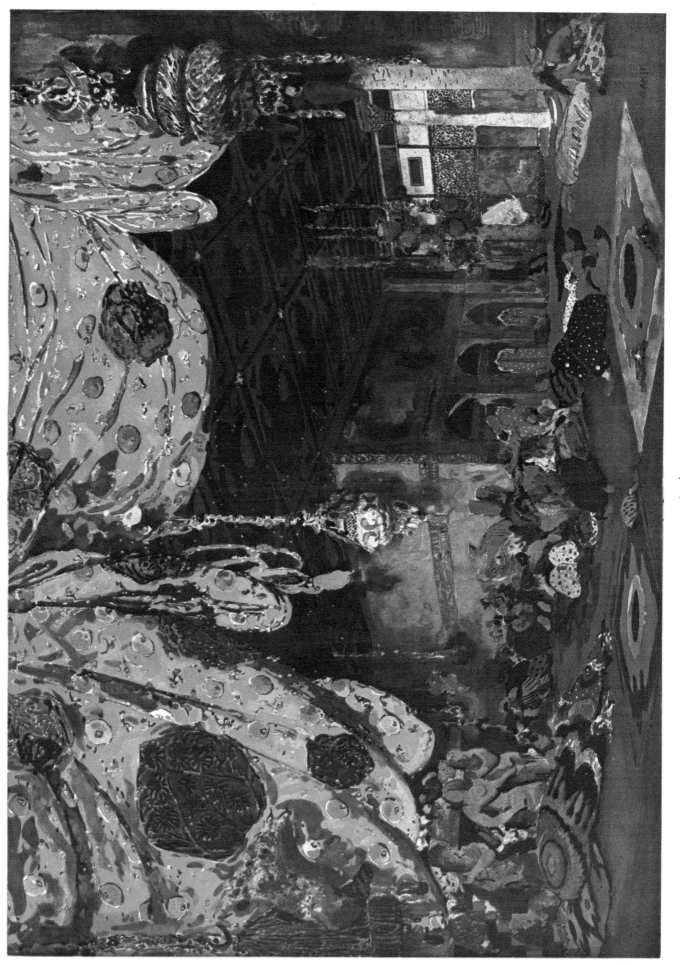

PLATE 27   SCHÉHÉRAZADE : Scenery

PLATE 28   SCHÉHÉRAZADE: Nègre Argent

PLATE 29   NARCISSE: A Bacchante

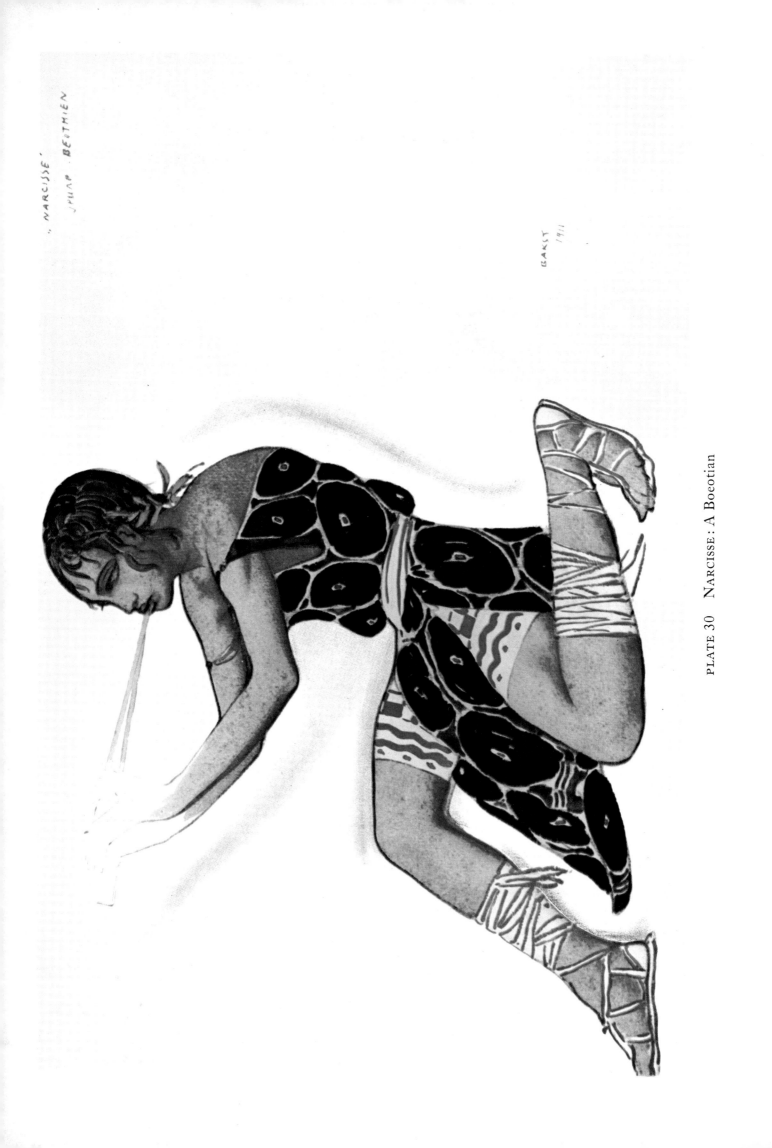

BAKST
1911

PLATE 30 NARCISSE: A Boeotian

PLATE 31   Narcisse : Two Bacchantes

PLATE 32   NARCISSE: A Youth

PLATE 33   Narcisse: First Bacchante

PLATE 34   NARCISSE : Scenery

PLATE 35　LA PÉRI: Title Rôle

PLATE 36 La Péri: Iskander (M. Nijinsky)

PLATE 37   SKETCH FOR A BALLET: Le Secret du Harem

PLATE 38   HÉLÈNE DE SPARTE : Hélène (Mme. Rubinstein)

PLATE 39   HÉLÈNE DE SPARTE : Scenery for Act III

PLATE 40   L'OISEAU DE FEU : Costume (Mme. Karsavina)

PLATE 41   Daphnis et Chloé: Scenery for Act I

PLATE 42   DAPHNIS ET CHLOÉ : Scenery for Act II

PLATE 43   DAPHNIS ET CHLOÉ: The Parting of Daphnis and Chloe (Act III)

PLATE 44   Daphnis et Chloé : Costume

PLATE 45   THAMAR: Scenery

PLATE 46   Fantaisie sur le Costume Moderne

PLATE 47   L'Averse (The Shower)

PLATE 48   AN INDIAN DANCER (La Marquise Casati)

PLATE 49   CLÉOPÂTRE: A Jewess

PLATE 50   CLÉOPÂTRE: A Jewish Dancer

PLATE 51   CLÉOPÂTRE: Bacchanale

PLATE 52   Schéhérazade: Nègre d'Or

PLATE 53   SCHÉHÉRAZADE: A Musician

PLATE 54   Narcisse: A Bacchante

« Il faut que chacun
tue son amour pour qu'il revive
sept fois plus ardent. »

Gabriele d'Annunzio

BAKST

„ST.SÉBASTIEN"
(mme IDA RUBINSTEIN)

PLATE 55   LE MARTYRE DE S. SÉBASTIEN : The Agony of St. Sebastian (Mme. Rubinstein)

PLATE 56   Le Martyre de S. Sébastien : Heralds

PLATE 57   LE MARTYRE DE S. SÉBASTIEN: The Agony of St. Sebastian (second idea)

PLATE 58 Le Martyre de S. Sébastien : Sketch of the Scenery for Act III

PLATE 59   Le Martyre de S. Sébastien : Scenery for Act IV

PLATE 60   HÉLÈNE DE SPARTE: First Sketch for Scenery (Act IV)

PLATE 61   HÉLÈNE DE SPARTE : Scenery for Act IV

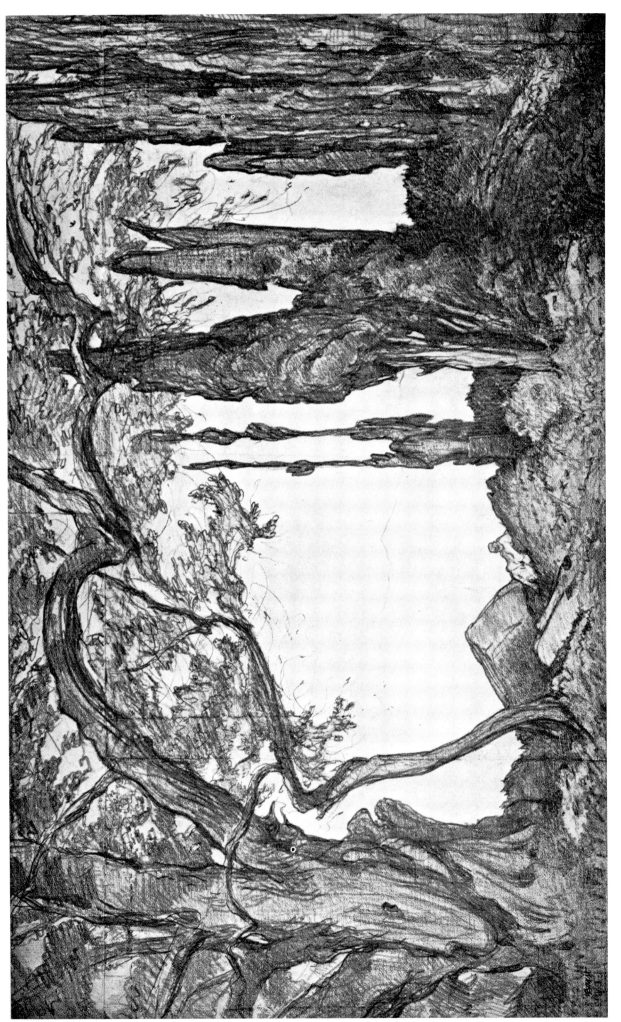

PLATE 62 HÉLÈNE DE SPARTE : Second Sketch for Scenery (Act IV)

PLATE 63   LE CARNAVAL: Harlequin (M. Nijinsky)

PLATE 64   LE CARNAVAL: Scenery

PLATE 65   LES PAPILLONS: Costume

PLATE 66 LES PAPILLONS: Costume

PLATE 67   LE SECRET DE SUZANNE : Scenery

PLATE 68   SALOMÉ : Title Rôle (Mme. Kouznetzov)

PLATE 69 DECORATIVE PANEL: Chloe Abandoned

PLATE 70   DECORATIVE PANEL: Elysium

PLATE 71   ILLUSTRATION FOR "THE NOSE" BY GOGOL

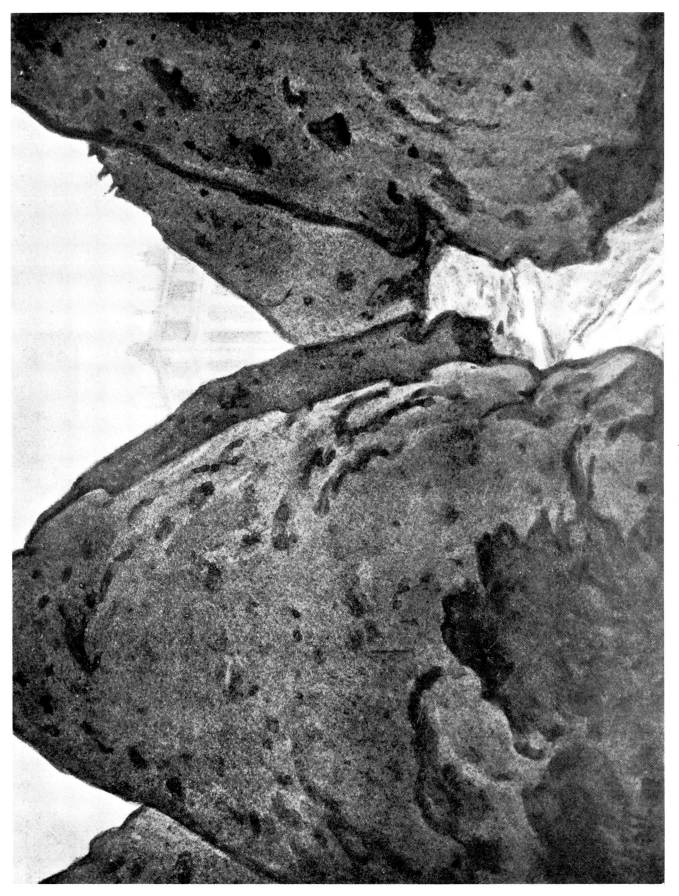

PLATE 72 Motif Décoratif (Versailles)

PLATE 73   PEN DRAWING: Le Nouveau Chemin

PLATE 74   TERROR ANTIQUUS

PLATE 75   TERROR ANTIQUUS (Detail)

PLATE 76   Terror Antiquus (Detail)

PLATE 77   VESTIBULE, DESIGNED BY BAKST, AT THE EXHIBITION OF
RUSSIAN ART AT THE AUTUMN SALON, 1906